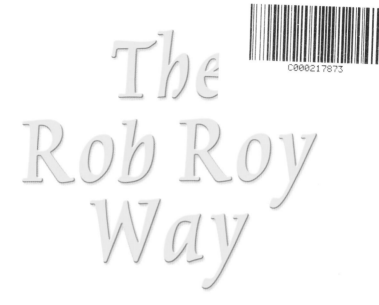

The Rob Roy Way

From Drymen to Pitlochry

Jacquetta Megarry

with

Rennie McOwan

Rucksack Readers

The Rob Roy Way: from Drymen to Pitlochry

Second edition published 2006 by Rucksack Readers, Landrick Lodge, Dunblane, FK15 0HY, UK

Telephone 01786 824 696 (+44 1786 824 696)
Fax   01786 825 090 (+44 1786 825 090)
Website   **www.rucsacs.com**
Email   **info@rucsacs.com**

Distributed in North America by Interlink Publishing, 46 Crosby Street, Northampton, Mass., 01060, USA
(www.interlinkbooks.com)

ISBN-13: 978-1-898481-26-3
ISBN-10: 1-898481-26-1

British Library cataloguing in publication data: a catalogue record for this book is available from the
British Library.

Designed by WorkHorse Productions (info@workhorse.co.uk)
Printed in China by Hong Kong Graphics and Printing Ltd
The maps in this book were created by Cartographic Consultants of Edinburgh © 2002, updated 2006
and based on Ordnance Survey mapping, on behalf of the Controller of Her Majesty's Stationery Office
© Crown Copyright, Licence No MC100039026

Publisher's note

Each walker is responsible for his or her own safety. The publisher cannot accept responsibility for ill-
health or injury, however caused. Walkers' rights and responsibilities are explained fully in the Scottish
Outdoor Access Code: see page 9.

The Rob Roy Way is an unofficial route devised by two walkers: see page 62. It has been followed
successfully by thousands of walkers since its launch in 2002 but it is not waymarked and unless you
are competent with map and compass you should not attempt to walk it alone. All information was
checked carefully in summer 2006, but before setting off walkers are advised to check two websites for
updates and diversions: **www.rucsacs.com/rrw/** and **www.robroyway.com**

Feedback is welcome and will be rewarded

Readers are encouraged to send comments (on the route and/or the book) to **info@rucsacs.com**.
All feedback will be acted upon, and anyone whose comments lead to changes will be entitled to claim
a free copy of our next edition upon publication.

The Rob Roy Way: contents

The graveyard at Balquhidder where Rob Roy is buried: see page 16

Foreword

Rob Roy MacGregor was always at home in the countryside of Scotland – a superb outdoorsman as well as an educated and intelligent man. Circumstances and ill fortune made him Scotland's most famous outlaw. His property was seized and his very surname proscribed for 40 years after his death. It is fitting that, over three centuries after his birth, a new Scottish long-distance walk has been named in his honour.

An expert at moving quickly over rough country, Rob Roy also proved to be a master of the art of escape. Despite being hunted down and arrested many times, he lived to the ripe old age of 63 and died peacefully in his bed. He was buried in the graveyard at Balquhidder, where the gravestone's legend is 'MacGregor despite them'.

This walk passes through many places where Rob Roy and his clansmen were active, especially around Aberfoyle and Killin. The route is steeped in clan history, Jacobite legends and tales of the Highlanders' resistance to government from London. The Way also features some interesting railway heritage and the Victorian Loch Katrine water scheme. This was the greatest achievement of municipal Scotland: it wiped out cholera overnight.

The Rob Roy Way has much to offer walkers from Scotland and abroad. It has been developed by walking enthusiasts making use of existing resources, without external funding or support. Although not an official Long Distance Route, this initiative demonstrates that long-distance walks can arise from the grass roots of walkers themselves. It deserves to be very popular.

The Rt Hon Sir David Steel (Lord Steel of Aikwood)

Part 1: Planning to walk the Way

The Rob Roy Way goes through many places strongly linked with Rob Roy MacGregor, Scotland's legendary outlaw: see page 14. In addition to its historic paths, railway heritage and glorious scenery, the Way is also rich in wildlife. And, of great practical importance to hungry and thirsty walkers, it links villages with friendly hosts and historic pubs.

The Clachan, Drymen, one of the Way's many fine pubs

You don't need to be an experienced long-distance walker to complete this hike. It is easier than the West Highland Way, for example, being shorter overall, less exposed and mainly on good terrain. However, it is not yet waymarked and in places you need to follow directions carefully. Be aware that nearly one-quarter of its 79 miles (126 km) involves road-walking. Although the roads are mostly minor, if you dislike walking on tarmac, consider choosing an official Long Distance Route instead: see page 63.

If you are inexperienced at walking, do not attempt the Way alone without having first learned to use a map and compass. Be aware that North is tilted on drop-down map panels 3-5. Well in advance of setting off on such a walk, you should complete a few long day hikes, to test your feet and gear.

No-one should undertake the Rob Roy Way casually, because the weather in Scotland is so unpredictable. On any given day, you may experience weather typical of any season, and perhaps of all four. This is all part of the experience, but also makes it important to have the right gear: see pages 11-12.

This book has been written for walkers following the recommended direction, from Drymen* to Pitlochry. The prevailing wind in Scotland is from the south-west, so you are more likely to have the wind at your back. Also, the more challenging parts are around Loch Tay, by which time you'll be well into your stride. Finally, on average there should be less rain as you move north-east. If walking in the opposite direction, reverse the instructions, noting various warnings about where turns would be easy to miss.

* For a pronunciation guide, see page 62.

How long will it take?

You can spread the walk over five to eight days, depending on the time available and the pace you find comfortable. Table 1 shows distances and overnight stops for the recommended seven-day schedule, and Part 3 describes the Way in seven sections. Table 2 shows how to save two days by starting from Aberfoyle and by-passing Callander. You can create six-day variations by doing one or other of these, or create your own itinerary using the map and website. For example, you could overnight in Lochearnhead and by-pass Killin, as explained on pages 46 and 48.

Table 1	miles	kilometres
Drymen		
	10	16
Aberfoyle		
	10	16
Callander		
	9	14
Strathyre		
	12	19
Killin		
	12	19
Ardtalnaig		
	15	24
Aberfeldy		
	11	18
Pitlochry		
Total	79	126

The Way fits comfortably over seven days

For those with more time, there's also an eight-day option which involves leaving the Way at Ardtalnaig and walking through Glen Almond and Glen Quaich, rejoining the Way again at the Birks of Aberfeldy: see page 57. This major extension is outside the scope of this book, but details will be found on the official website. Another variant is to begin at Milngavie, and follow the West Highland Way to Drymen.

Whichever approach you take, don't underestimate the time you need. If you feel under pressure you won't have time to linger over wildlife or to enjoy the fine scenery. Consider allowing further time for side-trips and perhaps some hill-climbing: see page 25. The suggested overnight stops reflect where accommodation and food are available. Don't leave accommodation to chance: it can be scarce out of season and in high summer, so pre-booking is essential. Refer to the official website and Tourist Information Centres: see page 61.

Table 2	miles	kilometres
Aberfoyle		
	16½	26
Strathyre		
	12	19
Killin		
	12	19
Ardtalnaig		
	15	24
Aberfeldy		
	11	18
Pitlochry		
Total	66½	106

The Way can be squeezed into five days if you start from Aberfoyle

Planning your travel

To plan your travel, consult the cover maps together with the table below. There is a good train service between Pitlochry and Glasgow or Edinburgh. Buses run frequently between Glasgow and Drymen, less often between Glasgow and Aberfoyle: see page 61. To reach the start and return from your finish points may need an extra overnight in or near Glasgow, Edinburgh or Pitlochry. Glasgow and Edinburgh are well-served by rail, road and air from elsewhere in the UK: see page 61. Glasgow International Airport is about 15 miles west of the city, whereas Glasgow Prestwick is about 30 miles south-west.

Table 3	miles	km	by bus	by train	by car
Glasgow / Pitlochry	80	129	2h 10m	1h 40m	1h 45m
Edinburgh / Pitlochry	75	121	2h	1h 45m	1h 45m
Glasgow / Edinburgh	48	77	1h	50m	1h
Glasgow / Drymen	18	29	1h	n/a	45m
Glasgow / Aberfoyle	26	42	1h 30m	n/a	1h

Distances and fastest journey times between selected places

Relying on public transport makes it easier to return unassisted to your starting-point. If you are in a group with a non-walking driver, arranging a rendez-vous with hikers is easy: each day's walk has contact points with roads. If you walk the Way in sections, please be very considerate about where you park. It is a major annoyance to land-owners, and can cause real hazards, if walkers leave cars in passing-places or obstructing gates. Please use the car parks provided, even when that means walking a little farther.

The table above shows the fastest scheduled times for bus and train (as of 2006). Car journeys are the best times likely within speed limits, not allowing for any traffic hold-ups or other stops. All figures are rough guidelines only: contact details are listed on page 61. Check schedules carefully in advance, as not all services are daily, and winter timetables are often restricted.

What is the best time of year?

Fortunately for those who have little choice, there is no bad time of year to walk the Way. You should be prepared for cold, wet and windy weather at any time. This book was researched and photographed mainly in winter, and revisited in all seasons. If you can walk at short notice, with the benefit of a weather forecast, winter may reward you with gin-clear visibility and more wildlife sightings.

Here are some factors to think about:

- Winter days are less flexible, because of the short hours of daylight: at this latitude they vary from 6-7 hours in late December to 17-18 in late June.
- Winter restricts your choice of side-trips, open mainly from April to October.
- Winter hikers are free from insect pests such as midges and clegs.
- On winter timetables, public transport is less frequent.
- In summer, more tourists are around and there is pressure on accommodation; however, in winter many B&Bs are closed for the season.

On balance, the ideal months are probably May/June and September/October. July and August are the busiest times both for tourists and midges. Having said that, much of the Way is very peaceful and rich in wildlife year-round. Take precautions if walking alone, especially on exposed sections: see page 25.

Walkers and land-owners

The Rob Roy Way has been developed by walking enthusiasts in collaboration with the relevant land-owners, who have been supportive. Any long-distance walk can strain this goodwill: a single careless walker can undermine the outcome of prolonged discussions, spoiling things for the considerate majority. Please consider yourself an ambassador for responsible walking at all times.

The Rob Roy Way has no official support and no budget for its maintenance. It takes advantage of existing resources, notably stretches of Cycle Route 7, but deviates from it in places and with good reason. About half lies on forestry tracks or open moorland, the forestry sections mainly owned by the Forestry Commission (FC). Excluding the Right of Way from Strathtay into Pitlochry and some sections of minor public road, you are walking on privately owned land.

Under the Scottish Outdoor Access Code, walkers' rights of responsible access to open country bring obligations to behave responsibly: see the panel below.

Killin 10

● ● ● ● ● ● ● ● ● ● ● ● ● ● ● ● ●

Common-sense and courtesy are a walker's best friends: remember that the countryside provides a livelihood for its residents. It may be your playground, but it is their workplace. Do not climb over fences or gates if there is a stile or any means of opening and re-fastening the gate. Take your litter away with you, and guard against all risk of fire. Help to safeguard water supplies and take care of wildlife, plants and trees.

Be very considerate of livestock. Stay well away from young lambs and their mothers, and never disturb pregnant ewes. Give cattle a wide berth, especially if they are with young. Read page 10 if you are thinking of taking a dog along.

During felling operations, the FC sometimes posts diversions: always follow local signage. For example, for many months during 2006 the section of forest track from Strathyre to Kingshouse was closed for clear-felling, and walkers had to stay on Cycle Route 7 via Balquhidder. In forests, be alert for timber traffic, especially on weekdays.

Deer-stalking is an important part of the rural economy for some estates. Without population control, deer numbers can increase explosively, leading to loss of habitat and death by starvation. Walkers should not disrupt deer stalking on the estates they walk through.

For roe deer stalking, the season is year-round (whether bucks or does) and the times to avoid are early morning and late evening, especially within an hour of sunrise and sunset. For red deer, the main season for stags is August to November, any day except Sunday, at any time of day. Please read the note on page 61 about stalking and the cross-country route from Killin to Ardeonaig.

Red deer stag

Dogs

The Way is generally suitable for dogs under proper control, although there is one cross-country section where the land-owner has objected to dogs: see page 49. You could use the minor road instead.

Think carefully before deciding to bring your pet along. Dogs must be kept under close control for their own safety. The notice shown here (photographed from the Way in Loch Ard Forest) is an extremist reference to a farmer's right, in some cases, to shoot your dog if it is attacking farm animals. Try to keep your dog well away from livestock, especially around lambing time (March to June). Obtain the excellent free leaflet *Walkies* from Scottish Natural Heritage (pubs@snh.gov.uk): it spells out what the SOAC means for dog owners.

Many farmers do not welcome visiting dogs

Cattle protect their young fiercely

If you are walking with your dog on the lead, keep well away from cattle: both dog and owner can be put in danger by this combination. Cattle protect their young fiercely, and may attack walkers, especially those with dogs. Serious injuries and even deaths have been caused by ignorance of this danger.

Finally, here are four practical points about taking your dog along:

1 If your dog fouls the path at any time, please clear up after it.
2 Some sections of the Way have tall ladder stiles where you will have to lift your dog over. This can be both strenuous and awkward, depending on the dog's weight and attitude.
3 Many accommodations do not accept dogs: check carefully before booking.
4 Dogs may disturb ground-nesting birds or young mammals: keep your dog under especially close control during the breeding season (April to June).

What to take with you

Review the packing list (pages 12-13) before deciding what to take along, and consider whether you need help with baggage-handling: see page 61 for details of the Bike & Hike service. If you are new to long-distance walking, consult our *Notes for novices*: see page 61 for details of how to obtain them. Also, consider the cautions on page 5 carefully.

Walkers in the Menteith Hills

Packing checklist

The checklist refers to your daytime needs only, and is divided into essential and desirable. Experienced walkers may disagree about what belongs in each category, but the list may still be a useful starting-point. Normally you will be wearing the first few items and carrying the rest in your rucksack.

Essential

- comfortable, waterproof walking boots and specialist socks
- breathable clothing, including full waterproofs
- hat and gloves
- water carrier and plenty of water (or purification tablets)
- enough food to last between supply points
- guidebook, compass and maps: see page 62
- blister treatment and first aid kit
- insect repellent: in summer months, expect midges (small biting insects), ticks and/or clegs (horse-flies), especially in still weather
- waterproof rucksack cover or liner, e.g. bin (garbage) bag
- enough cash in pounds sterling for the week.

Cash is suggested because credit cards are not always acceptable and cash machines are not common along the Way. Bin bags have many uses, e.g. storing wet clothing or preventing hypothermia: cut holes for your head and arms.

Desirable

- compass, large-scale maps, whistle and torch: essential if you are doing any 'serious' side-trips or hiking in winter
- pole(s)
- binoculars: useful for navigation and spotting wildlife
- camera, ideally light and rugged; take spare batteries and memory cards/film
- pouch or secure pockets: to keep small items handy but safe
- gaiters, to keep mud and water away from boots and trousers
- toilet tissue (biodegradable)
- weather (sun and wind) protection for eyes and skin
- water purification tablets
- spare socks: changing socks at lunchtime can relieve damp feet
- spare shoes (e.g. trainers), spare bootlaces
- notebook and pen.

If you are camping, you will need much more gear, including tent, groundsheet, sleeping mat and sleeping bag. You may also need a camping stove, cooking utensils and food. If you are carrying everything on your back, you will need to be strong, experienced and well-organised.

Two final issues: first, where should you 'go' if caught short on the Way? The official advice is

- Use public toilets where available.
- If you need to relieve yourself out of doors, pass water well away from streams, paths and water courses.
- Excrement poses health risks, and is unpleasant for others. If you have to go, choose a discreet spot at least 50 yards away from streams, paths and any buildings, preferably further. If possible, bury waste in a deep hole; some people carry a trowel for the purpose.

The second is what about mobile phones? You should not rely on one for personal safety: reception may be poor or non-existent. For updated information on network coverage from different providers, check the website **www.robroyway.com**.

2·1 Rob Roy and the Jacobites

Rob Roy MacGregor, the third son of Donald Glas MacGregor of Glengyle and Margaret Campbell, was born in Glengyle, on Loch Katrineside, in 1671. He spent much of his life in the Trossachs, the area of lochs and rugged hills lying east of Loch Lomond. From Aberfoyle to Killin, the Way skirts the eastern edge of the Trossachs.

Rob Roy was a man of property and was involved in large-scale cattle droving and dealing. He and his brother Iain developed the Lennox Watch, a body that offered 'protection' to cattle owners in return for money. When protection money was not paid, cattle tended mysteriously to 'disappear'. Activities like this by the MacGregors and some other clans gave us the word 'blackmail', *black* for nefarious deeds and the colour of most of the cattle of past times; *mail* from Scots and Gaelic words for rent or payment. (The larger, and mainly red-brown Highland cows that we see today are a 19th century cross-breed.)

Highland cattle used to be black, long-horned and long-haired (like this modern animal), but smaller

After his father was captured and imprisoned, Rob Roy effectively became the Chief of a leading section of his pugnacious and persecuted clan, aged only 30. In those days the powerful Duke of Montrose was his patron.

His luck changed and his business collapsed when his head drover left, taking the enormous sum of £1000, all the money intended for cattle purchase. In 1712 the Duke of Montrose (to whom he owed money) turned against him and had him bankrupted and outlawed. His wife and family were evicted and several of his houses were burned or ransacked.

Rob Roy swore vengeance, and took to the hills in a long campaign of thieving cattle, occasionally kidnapping Montrose's servants and swiping his enemies. His frequent escapes, popularity with local people and generosity to the poor all gained him a reputation as a Scottish Robin Hood. Unlike the legendary Robin, Rob Roy's life is well-documented and factual: see page 62 for references to some biographical sources.

In all, he and his family lived in seven houses; two on Loch Katrine-side, two in Balquhidder and one each in Glen Dochart, Glen Shira (in Argyll) and on Loch Lomond-side. Most were ransacked or burned on occasion, and in addition he used a network of caves and hidey-holes.

A fine example lies on a promontory in Loch Ard-side, about 4 km west of Aberfoyle. Maps, including the FC map mentioned on page 61, show this at grid reference 481 014, at the north-eastern edge of a promontory. From the lochside forest track, it takes ten minutes to follow the path northward and scramble down to this atmospheric jumble of overgrown caves and crannies, making an interesting side-trip from Aberfoyle. Allow half an hour to reach the cave from the B829 road at Milton.

Many stories arose from Rob Roy's fighting strength and striking appearance, with his fiery red hair: *Roy* comes from the Gaelic *ruadh*, meaning red. His air of command was backed up by impressive qualities of leadership. He was romanticised in the novels of Sir Walter Scott who claimed Rob had very long arms, but there is no confirmation of that.

Statue that stands in Stirling city centre, donated by Adam McGregor Dick of Kilmarnock, a direct descendant of Rob Roy's

He mobilised most of Clan Gregor on the Jacobite side (see page 17) and took part in the Battle of Sheriffmuir in November 1715. He was accused of treason because of his Jacobite activities.

The Duke of Montrose captured him at Balquhidder in 1717, but he made a daring escape while fording the River Forth en route to Stirling Castle. He was recaptured by the Duke of Atholl in Dunkeld and imprisoned in Logierait, but he escaped again after only one night. Eventually, with support from the Duke of Argyll, he received the King's pardon in 1725.

He died in his bed at Inverlochlarig nine years later, and was buried in the Kirkton of Balquhidder where his wife and two of his sons were also later interred. There was a massive attendance at his funeral. He had outwitted two dukes and the British Army, and much that was good in the life of the old Highlands went with his passing.

The grave's legend 'MacGregor despite them' is a defiant response to the Hanoverian Government's attempt to destroy the clan by forbidding the use of the MacGregor surname. This prevented them from entering into legal contracts, and it happened on several occasions. The most recent prohibition was lifted in 1775, and the memory of the old MacGregors, the Children of the Mist, lives on to this day.

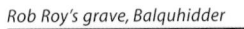
Rob Roy's grave, Balquhidder

The gravestone legend defiantly asserts the surname

MacGREGOR DESPITE THEM

Chronology

1671	Rob Roy MacGregor was born in Glengyle on Loch Katrine-side
1689	Battle of Killicrankie was won by the Jacobites, at which Rob Roy and his father fought on the successful side in the first campaign of the Jacobite cause. The MacGregor surname was proscribed by William of Orange as a result.
1693	Rob Roy married his cousin, Mary MacGregor of Comer.
1702	William of Orange died; Anne succeeded as Queen.
1707	Union of Scottish and English Parliaments took place.
1712	Rob Roy was made bankrupt by the Duke of Montrose after an aide absconded with his funds, and he was declared an outlaw.
1713	Montrose's men evict Rob Roy's family, and they moved to Glen Dochart. Rob Roy was sheltered in Finlarig Castle, Killin for a while.
1714	Queen Anne died, and was succeeded by George I under the Act of Settlement, 1701.
1715	First Jacobite uprising ends indecisively after the Battle of Sheriffmuir, 13 November 1715.
1717	Rob Roy was captured at Balquhidder, escaped while crossing the Forth, was recaptured in Dunkeld, imprisoned in Logierait, and promptly escaped again.
1720	Rob Roy moved to Inverlochlarig in Balquhidder Glen.
1725	Rob Roy submitted to King George I via General Wade.
1730	Rob Roy converted to Catholicism at Drummond Castle.
1734	Rob Roy died at Inverlochlarig and was buried at Balquhidder.

The Jacobites

In 1688, James VII of Scotland (who also became James II of England after the Union of the Crowns in 1603) was deposed by popular demand, largely because he was thought to be promoting the Catholic Church. His Protestant daughter Mary was enthroned instead, along with her Dutch husband, the Protestant William of Orange.

Those who continued to support the direct Stuart line of James VII and his son James (the 'Old Pretender') became known as Jacobites: *Jacobus* is Latin for James. The unpopularity of the 1707 Treaty of Union, together with the sense of distance from decisions made in London, gave the Jacobite cause a nationalist flavour. Additionally, most Jacobites were Roman Catholics or Episcopalians, and Highland Jacobites felt that the Gaelic way of life was under threat.

During 1689-1745, contact was kept up between Scotland and the exiled Jacobite court, first in France and then in Italy. The two most famous

Wade's favourite bridge, Aberfeldy, built in 1733

Jacobite risings took place in 1715 and 1745. The 'Fifteen' focused on the Old Pretender and effectively ended after the Battle of Sheriffmuir in November 1715. Although the Jacobites heavily outnumbered the Government forces, they failed to win a conclusive victory.

However, Jacobite discontent continued to flourish in the Highlands. A small Rising took place in 1719 when the Jacobite clans, including Rob Roy, were joined by a contingent of Spaniards, but it fizzled out after a short battle in Glen Shiel, in the western Highlands. It gave us one of our most interesting hill names, Sgurr nan Spainteach, the Spaniards' Peak. The next main rising, the 'Forty-five', focussed on the Old Pretender's son, Charles Edward Stuart, also known as 'Bonnie Prince Charlie'.

Although warmly acclaimed on arrival in Scotland from France, his march southward into England gained so little support there that the Jacobites retreated and hoped to hold 'Fortress Scotland' until more French aid came. The Battle of Culloden in 1746 marked their final defeat. However, 'Bonnie Prince Charlie' remained in Scotland for another five months, living in hiding, and being pursued all over the Highlands and islands by the military.

In those unsettled times, Government control of the Highlands depended on good communications, intensive patrolling and key forts. A leading figure in this was General George Wade (1673-1748), Commander-in-Chief of the Hanoverian army in North Britain (i.e. Scotland). During 1724-40, he and his subordinate, Major William Caulfeild, built 240 miles of military roads and many forts and barracks in the Highlands. From the Way just north of Lochearnhead, you can see traces of a military road running parallel to the railway trackbed, to its east. This was built in 1751 by Caulfeild's men.

Although Wade is famous for his military roads, he himself thought his finest achievement was the Tay bridge in Aberfeldy. It was built to a design of William Adam's, and after over 250 years it still carries vehicles without any weight restriction, thanks to its superb design and construction.

2·2 Other history

Loch Katrine water scheme

The Loch Katrine water scheme was a bold response to the lack of clean drinking water for the rapidly expanding city of Glasgow. In the nineteenth century, private water companies sold water to the public from horse carts, and diseases flourished. The cholera outbreaks of 1838 and 1848 resulted in many thousands of deaths. In 1853 the city fathers commissioned John Bateman, a civil engineer, to look at options for improving the water supply. He reported that the best source was Loch Katrine: there was very heavy rainfall in its catchment area and also its water was exceptionally pure.

An Act of Parliament (1855) was needed to authorise the engineering works. These were on an impressive scale:

- a huge dam to raise the level of Loch Katrine
- an aqueduct 26 miles (42 km) long to carry the water towards Glasgow
- a storage reservoir at Mugdock, just to the north of Glasgow
- 26 miles (42 km) of mains aqueduct and 46 miles (74 km) of distribution pipes to deliver the water to households throughout the city.

The Way passes to the right of the 1859 Corrie Aqueduct (looking north)

Astonishingly, these works were completed in under four years, and in October 1859 Queen Victoria opened the scheme. It was a resounding success, wiping out cholera at a stroke.

The scheme was extended by a further Act of Parliament in 1885, and a second 'new' aqueduct constructed between 1886 and 1903. Thanks to improved tunnelling techniques, this was slightly shorter than the first, with a faster flow rate. The Way follows the route of the 1859 aqueduct closely in Loch Ard forest: see diagram below. Even before you reach the Corrie Aqueduct, you can trace its route underground by looking out for its rounded stone markers, as shown in this photograph.

Development continued when further catchment areas were connected directly to that of Loch Katrine. Loch Arklet was completed in 1914 and Glen Finglas only in 1965.

The build quality of the original works is impressive, and you pass several superb structures on your way through Loch Ard forest. The stonework of the ventilation shafts speaks of Victorian pride in their design and construction: see page 35. Walking alongside the magnificent Corrie Aqueduct, you may wonder how many modern structures will still be working as well in 150 years time.

Nowadays, when full the reservoirs hold about twelve days' water supply for the City of Glasgow and its environs. Over a million people still enjoy the legacy of this bold and enlightened scheme of Victorian engineering.

The aqueducts in Loch Ard forest

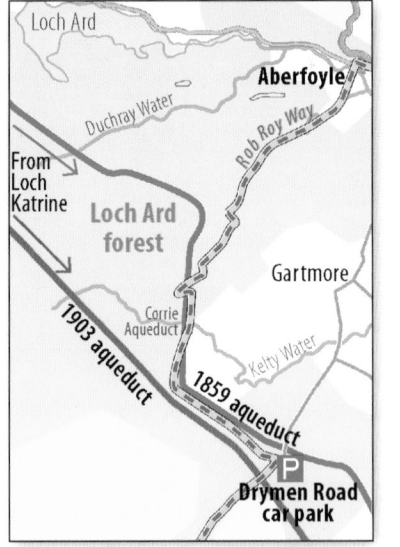

Lochearnhead station

The railway heritage

From Callander to the top of Glen Ogle, the Way follows the trackbed of the Callander and Oban Line, constructed to link the fast-growing city of Glasgow with the Highland port of Oban via Dunblane, Callander and Kingshouse. Ever since Scott's novels had first made Scotland popular, romantic Victorians (including the Queen herself) were visiting in increasing numbers. The expansion of the railways encouraged this trend.

The long haul up Glen Ogle was at a gradient of 1 in 60, over an impressive viaduct built in 1870. The line was completed to Oban in 1880. It was operated from the outset by the Caledonian Railway, which became part of the London Midland and Scottish in 1923. After nationalisation in 1948, the line continued until sadly it closed in September 1965. Doomed by the Beeching report, its closure was brought forward by a serious rock fall.

A separate branch of the Caledonian Railway had joined Perth to Crieff in 1867. This was extended westward to St Fillans in 1901 and to Lochearnhead in 1904, joining the Oban line at Balquhidder Junction in 1905. This last section was expensive to construct because of the heavy rock tunnelling and two large viaducts, one of which you see clearly from the high part of the Way when looking south towards the village of Lochearnhead.

Sadly, this line lasted less than 50 years, and after it closed in 1951 the track was removed. The Lochearnhead station buildings fell into disrepair, until the Hertfordshire Scouts (based some 400 miles to the south) saw its potential as an outdoor centre. Their bold fund-raising efforts allowed them first to lease it and then in 1977 to buy it to secure its future. As the photograph shows, the station has been beautifully restored. If you divert from the Way into Lochearnhead (see page 46) you pass the entrance to this Scout Station and can see its platform and buildings.

Further north, the Killin Railway Company opened its line in March 1886, linking the Callander & Oban line to Killin village and its steamer service on Loch Tayside. The Marquis of Breadalbane was a major sponsor of this tiny independent company, and many local people were also persuaded to support it. The service was operated by the Caledonian Railway, but it was hopelessly uneconomic. Its shareholders were fortunate indeed to get their money back after the affair of the stolen clock: see panel. The Killin line finally closed in September 1965.

i
The stolen station clock
Under the 1923 Act of Parliament that grouped the many small British railways into the 'big four', the Caledonian Railway fell under the London, Midland and Scottish (LMS) grouping. By mistake, the tiny Killin company was overlooked by the draftsmen. The LMS behaved as if it owned it, and LMS officials removed the Killin station clock to instal it at Euston. As a result, the Killin company took legal action, and a generous settlement ensued, sparing the LMS huge embarrassment. The clock remained at Euston for 40 years.

The Way runs along the Glenogle viaduct, 1870

Pre-history around Loch Tay

In the simplest terms, pre-history since about 4500 BC can be divided into three periods:

- the Neolithic period until about 2200 BC, when the nomadic way of life gave way to farming
- the Bronze Age, from 2200 BC until about 800-600 BC, when bronze was used for making tools and weapons
- the Iron Age, when iron took over from bronze as the prime metal, from about 600 BC until the early centuries AD.

The wooded shores of Loch Tay and the flatter lands of Strath Tay to its north-east have been inhabited since pre-historic times. You see many signs of this on the map and from the Way: crannogs (see below), forts, standing stones, tumuli (burial mounds) and mysterious cup and ring marked rocks.

Kenmore is a great centre for exploring the pre-historic remains of this area. Croft Moraig is the most complete stone circle of its kind in Scotland. It stands 2½ miles (4 km) north-east of Kenmore next to the A827 on its south side (grid reference NN 797 472). Access is via a swing gate at the corner of the farm track. Although not in public care, it is in good condition and well worth a visit. Thought to be at least 4000 years old, it is even more ancient than the simple four-post circle that the Way passes above Strathtay village: see page 59.

Croft Moraig stone circle, near Kenmore

The Scottish Crannog Centre

Crannogs are an ancient type of loch-dwelling found throughout Scotland and Ireland. There are 18 crannogs in Loch Tay alone. People went on occupying them periodically from 3000 BC until as recently as the 17th century AD.

Crannogs were built out in the water to be secure from invaders and wild animals; some were symbols of status or power. Many were originally timber-built round houses, supported on stilts driven into the loch bed. Today what you see are submerged stony mounds or tree-covered islands.

The Scottish Crannog Centre is focussed on its reconstructed Oakbank Crannog which is 2600 years old. This was based on the nearby early Iron Age site in Loch Tay which divers have been excavating since 1980. In addition to the guided tours, there are audiovisual displays, events and hands-on demonstrations of ancient skills such as wool-spinning, grain-grinding and fire-making.

The Centre is five minutes walk south-west of Kenmore and is open daily from mid-March to October from 10.00 to 17.30 (weekends only, 10.00 to 16.00 in November). There is a small admission charge: tel 01887 830 583. Visit its website at **www.crannog.co.uk**.

The Scottish Crannog Centre, near Kenmore

2·3 Munros, Corbetts and Grahams

A Munro is a Scottish mountain whose summit is over 3000 feet (914 m), provided its peak is adequately separate from any neighbouring Munros: without a 500-foot drop between them it will be classified as a mere 'Top'.

They are named after Hugh Munro, a London-born doctor (1856-1919). His published table (1891) listed 238 such peaks (and 538 Tops). There has been protracted debate about the total, and the exact distinction between a Munro and a Top, ever since. The Scottish Mountaineering Club's 1997 figure is 284 Munros and 511 Tops, the revised numbers reflecting more accurate survey methods.

The first 'Munroist' was the Reverend A E Robertson, who completed his final Munro (as then listed) in 1901. Since then, 'Munro-bagging' has become a popular sport. Some determined climbers ascend them all in a single expedition lasting several months, whereas others spread the challenge over a lifetime. Charlie Campbell, a Glasgow postman, set a most impressive record of 48½ days in July 2000. At least 100 people become Munroists every year, and thousands of people are working on their personal lists as you read this.

Ben Vorlich and Stuc a' Chroin from Glen Ogle

Mountain Code

Before you go

Learn the use of map and compass.

Know the weather signs and local forecast.

Plan within your abilities.

Know simple first aid and the symptoms of exposure.

Know the mountain distress signals.

When you go

Never go alone.

Leave a note of your route, and report on your return.

Take windproofs, waterproofs and survival bag.

Take suitable map and compass, torch and food.

Wear climbing boots.

Keep alert all day.

In winter

(November to March)

Each person needs an ice-axe and crampons, and to know how to use them.

The group needs climbing rope, and to know how to use it.

Learn to recognise dangerous snow slopes.

To report an accident on the mountains, telephone the police on 01786 456 000 (Drymen to Loch Tay) or 01796 472 222 (Loch Tay to Pitlochry) and ask for Mountain Rescue

Lochan Breachlaich from Creag Gharbh

Throughout the Way, your views are dominated by various Munros: the most southerly is Ben Lomond, whose peak you glimpse from Loch Ard forest. Looking back down Glen Ogle, you see the twin peaks of Ben Vorlich and Stuc a' Chroin: see photographs on pages 25 and 46. Approaching Killin you will see the Tarmachan ridge (page 49) and along Loch Tay-side the view is dominated by the Lawers group. Ben Lawers is Perthshire's highest mountain at 3984 feet (1214 m). Beyond the northern end of Loch Tay, notice the distinctive ridge of Schiehallion (3547 feet, 1083 m): see page 53. Experiments on this isolated, symmetrical mountain in the eighteenth century led Charles Hutton to develop the concept of contour lines.

A Corbett is smaller than a Munro: it is over 2500 feet (762 m) and has a drop of at least 500 feet all round. There are several Corbetts close to the Way, notably Ben Ledi (2875 feet, 879 m) which dominates the town of Callander. The Way passes the start of one path to its summit: see page 43.

Never underestimate Ben Ledi: it has dangerous slopes on its eastern face and snow often lies late. Although it is partly waymarked, you need compass skills if mist descends. On a fine day, the views from its summit are excellent in all directions. There's a fine round trip, climbing from the Stank car park and, after the summit, heading on north to descend via Stank Glen. Allow about four hours for this.

Grahams are defined in metric units: over 610 m (2001 feet) and with a drop of at least 150 m (492 feet) all round. There are many Grahams near the Way, including Creag Gharbh (637 m), whose shoulder you traverse east of Lochan Breachlaich.

2·4 Habitats and wildlife

The Rob Roy Way runs through three main types of habitat, described below:

- water-side
- woodland
- heath and moorland.

To improve your chances of wildlife sightings, carry binoculars and walk alone, or with fellow-walkers who share your interest and are willing to move quietly. Try to set off soon after sunrise, or go for a stroll in the evening. Animals are much more active at these times than in the middle of the day. Since this applies to midges too, protect your skin thoroughly, especially from May to September and in still weather.

Water-side

Much of the Way passes near water, alongside various lochs, rivers and falls. Look out for grey heron standing motionless in the shallows, hunting for fish and frogs. In flight they trail their legs, and their huge wings beat very slowly. They need tall trees to nest in.

Grey heron nesting, with chicks

Watch for signs of otter, such as spraints on rocks and river banks, or the remains of frog skins or fish. They are shy and easily disturbed, but their population is rising around quiet sheltered river banks.

Oystercatchers are easy to spot: look for their white-on-black M-shape in flight, and listen for their shrill piercing cries. Their long orange-red bills are good at cracking open molluscs. In winter, they congregate around estuaries, but from March to July they move inland to breed, often nesting in fields.

Near streams and rapids, look out for the dipper, a starling-sized bird with aquatic tendencies. This athletic bird often stands or walks in fast-moving rivers, plunging in fearlessly to feed on tiny fish, molluscs and tadpoles. Recognise dippers by their shape and colour: white throat and chest, with mainly black body and brownish head.

Woodland

The Rob Roy Way goes through large areas of forest, mainly productive conifers with some semi-natural woodland. The Forestry Commission (FC) owns most of this land, and is re-structuring the conifer woodlands whilst expanding and linking the remnants of older broadleaved woodland. This involves planting native broadleaved trees, removing exotic conifers and controlling invasive rhododendrons.

Dipper feeding from a fast-moving stream

Barn owl

As the mature woodlands are harvested, the FC takes the opportunity to diversify the range of tree species and to break up the age structure of the forests. More spaces are being cleared, particularly along watercourses, lowering the tree line on hillsides and revealing natural features and archaeological sites.

Woodland provides food, nesting sites and shelter for wildlife. The fragile barn owl population has increased, mainly due to a long-term FC nest box scheme in the Loch Ard Forest area, and also thanks to its woodland re-structuring. Although nocturnal, barn owls hunt in the last hour before dusk and sometimes in the early morning, particularly if they have young to feed. They prefer open woodland, farmland or moorland with plenty of long grass.

Wild primrose flourishing in birch woodland

Pine martens live in woodland

The pine marten became almost extinct in Britain and is therefore a protected species. Its rapid population rise in the southern Highlands reflects the increase in woodland. They are regularly found breeding in some of the barn owl boxes. The pine marten is the only mammal that is agile enough to catch red squirrels.

In spring, the woodland floor may be carpeted with bluebells or wood sorrel, and many other wild flowers flourish, such as primrose, violet and celandine. Scotland has 75% of the British red squirrel population, and coniferous forests are a good place to look for them. If you see chewed-up cones lying on the ground, look about for the red squirrels that may have been feeding on them recently.

Red squirrel in spruce tree

Roe deer partly hidden by bracken

Britain has only two native species of deer: red and roe, both of which originally lived in woodland. Red deer (see page 10) subsequently adapted to life on open upland, but their smaller cousin, the roe deer, never made the transition. Although normally shy, you may see them almost anywhere along the Way, especially if you walk alone or quietly. Once they have seen or heard you, all you will see is the kidney-shaped white patch on their fast-disappearing rumps.

Heath and moorland

Examples of Scots pine are found along various parts of the Way, especially on poor soils and in exposed places, high above Loch Tay. After the Ice Age, 8 to 10 thousand years ago,

Scots pine re-colonised Scotland, and it is the only pine tree native to Britain. Isolated trees are useful perches for birds of prey. Mature trees have a distinctive shape and strongly patterned bark.

Scots pine (Pinus sylvestris) has a distinctive shape (above) and strongly patterned bark (left)

Look up and you may see various birds of prey, including tawny and barn owls, which mainly depend on small mammals for their diet. Field voles live on grass, plants and fruit, and are an important part of the food chain: eight different species of bird, as well as several mammals, prey upon it. As much as 90% of the barn owl's diet consists of field voles, so it is vulnerable to any drop in this population.

You have a good chance of seeing buzzard, a large bird of prey, and widespread in Scotland. It feeds on small mammals, especially rabbits. Typically you will see buzzard soaring and circling on air currents, its wings held motionless in a shallow Vee, watching for prey with its sharp eyes. They may make a distinctive mewing call, especially in the breeding season, and sometimes they perch on tree stumps or even fence-posts.

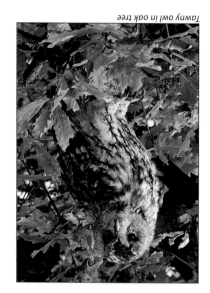

Tawny owl in oak tree

Buzzard feeding on rabbit

Black grouse

The buzzard is also known as 'the tourist's eagle', because visitors to Scotland so often mistake it for eagle. The golden eagle's wing-span is over six feet, double the buzzard's, and it is confined to more remote areas. If you ever see one, it will be far away, perhaps soaring high above the heather: consider yourself very lucky.

Watch and listen for grouse – large, ground-nesting game birds which make distinctive loud calls and, when disturbed, take off with an explosive whirring of wings. Red grouse favour open heather moorland, whereas black grouse prefer a mixture of this with woodland. On the higher ground, you might also see ptarmigan, a mountain grouse whose body feathers turn white in winter.

Tender young oak leaves

3·1 Drymen to Aberfoyle

Map	**panel 1**
Distance	**10 miles (16 km)**
Terrain	**minor road then forest tracks with some tarmac, followed by minor road and pavements into Aberfoyle**
Grade	**mostly easy or very easy, maximum height 500 ft (150 m)**
Food and drink	**Drymen, Aberfoyle**
Side-trips	**Scottish Wool Centre and Trossachs Discovery Centre, both in Aberfoyle**
Summary	**pleasant sheltered walk mainly on forest track, passing many Victorian water supply features**

- The Way leaves Drymen's main square by a minor road, going north past the Clachan Inn and soon passing Drymen Primary School. A mile later, the West Highland Way crosses this minor road, but you continue straight on.

- Follow the undulating minor road for a further couple of miles as far as the Drymen Road car park. There are fine views to your right of the Campsie Fells, with the volcanic plug of Dumgoyne at their southern end.

- From the highest point of the road, look north-east, the white houses of Gartmore contrasting with the dark craggy Menteith Hills behind Aberfoyle. After passing a tall radio mast, the road descends for a further mile to reach Drymen Road car park, which is on the right.

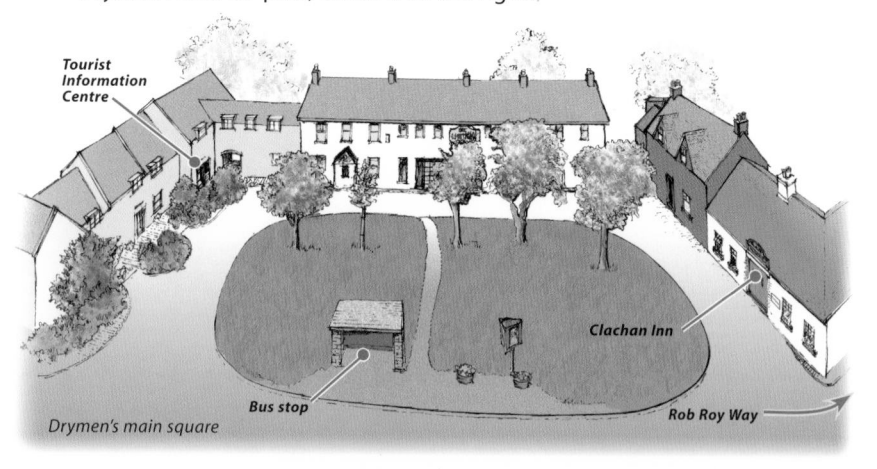

Tourist Information Centre

Clachan Inn

Bus stop

Rob Roy Way

Drymen's main square

The Way passes several of these domed shafts

- Opposite the car park, turn left off the road into Loch Ard forest. Two roads enter the forest here: take the one bearing right (north-west), with a warning notice about maximum weight – for forestry vehicles, not walkers. From time to time you will glimpse the summit of Ben Lomond ahead to the north-west.

- Follow this forest road for the next 3 miles (5 km), through intermittent woodland with many clearings. The surface is smooth tarmac at first, giving way to a looser surface with pot-holes after the Corrie Aqueduct. To your right, the views feature Ben Ledi to the north-east and Ben Venue just west of north, with the dark rolling Menteith Hills in the foreground.

- You are walking through part of the huge Loch Katrine water scheme. Look for the rounded stones on your right that trace the line of the 1856-9 aqueduct, here running in a tunnel beneath your feet: see pages 19-20.

- After ten minutes you pass a couple of houses, with the first of several domed shafts on your left. These were used for extracting spoil and for ventilation, and are a feature of today's walk. On your right, look for the covered aqueduct with walkway above, running into its tunnel.

Drymen — $3^3/_4$ 6 — Drymen Road car park — $3^3/_4$ 6 — Clashmore Cottage — $2^1/_2$ 4 — Aberfoyle

The Way turns right at the second domed shaft

- The road now swings northward. After a further five minutes, it reaches the impressive Corrie Aqueduct, dating from 1859 and still in fine working order. At the junction just before it, bear right on the minor track (which may appear blocked by a low barrier). Walk north alongside the Aqueduct, keeping it on your left: see photograph and map on pages 19-20.

- Shortly (500 m) after the Aqueduct, the forest track starts to hairpin uphill, crossing and re-crossing under the electricity pylons. Ignore a cycle track that joins from the right, then leaves from the left, instead following the main track uphill until it levels out. Looking south you may see fine views of the Campsies, terminating in the volcanic plug of Dumgoyne.

- Looking ahead (north), you will see three domed shafts below you, one nearby and two further away, vertically in line. The middle one marks an important junction: see photograph above.

- Turn right at this junction and re-enter the forest, crossing a stream and continuing for one further mile (1½ km) of gentle descent.

- At the next important junction, Clashmore Cottage, turn sharp left uphill (north-west).
- Within five minutes you reach a complicated 5-way junction where you bear right (north-east). You are joined by a stream (the Bofrishlie Burn) that leads downhill and eventually into the Forth. Follow this road for the final two miles out of the forest, ignoring various other minor tracks that join it from right and left.
- You emerge from the forest at Balleich, following the minor road for a further mile into Aberfoyle. Halfway along this section, note Kirkton Church and Cemetery on your right. Near the church entrance, there are two 'mort-safes' – cast-iron coffins made heavy to discourage body snatchers. The information board explains more about the church's interesting history.
- On arrival in Aberfoyle, turn right at the A821 main road for the village centre, or turn into the car park just beforehand for the Tourist Information Centre and Scottish Wool Centre.

i

Scottish Wool Centre
Visitor centre, shop and restaurant with sheepdog demonstrations (herding Indian Runner Ducks). 'The story of Scottish wool' (admission charge) features rare sheep, shearing and spinning. Open daily year-round, tel 01877 382 850.

i

Trossachs Discovery Centre
Tourist Information Centre with free audiovisual about the Trossachs and its history, helpful staff and well-stocked shop. Open daily March-October, also weekends year-round, tel 01877 382 352.

Looking west over Aberfoyle towards Ben Lomond

River Teith, Callander

If short of time, you could combine sections 3.2 and 3.3 to walk 16.5 miles (26 km) from Aberfoyle to Strathyre – see page 41.

Map	panels 1 and 2
Distance	10 miles (16 km)
Terrain	mainly forest track, some stony path with several streams to cross, sometimes boggy underfoot; forest road, then minor road into Callander
Grade	first half mainly easy, maximum height 725 ft (220 m); last three miles flat
Food and drink	Aberfoyle, Callander, also Kilmahog
Side-trips	Rob Roy Centre, Callander (see page 41)
Summary	glorious walk through the Menteith hills, followed by a descent to Loch Venachar with fine views to the north

- Leave Aberfoyle's main car park by walking east past the Scottish Wool Centre (on your right) on to a path signed Cycle Route 7.
- Follow this (the trackbed of an old railway) for 250 yards, then bear left towards the main road at a grass triangle.
- Cross the road and continue along its pavement to the health centre, where the Way turns left up a minor road signed for 'Dounans Outdoor Centre'. Walk uphill straight past the Centre, keeping its buildings on your left.
- Just beyond the small pond, you meet a forest road at a T-junction where you turn right. The road gradually gains height, lined by stately tall trees. Look back for picturesque views over Aberfoyle Golf Course to the distant hills beyond.
- Follow the track, keeping straight on past a signpost to Braeval car park where a road joins from the left. After 250 yards, at a T-junction which also has a sign down to Braeval, turn left up the forestry road.
- As you gain height, the hills on the left become more rugged. At the end of the forest, cross a small stream before a wall. You reach a platform stile, but in recent years you could simply walk around it, passing through a gap in the wall to enter the Malling Forestry Estate.
- The terrain becomes rougher as the stony path meanders over the Menteith Hills. You cross several streams and another fence (by ladder stile) to reach a splendid open stretch across rough pasture. In places the path becomes less distinct, mingling with sheep tracks. SImply keep walking north-east and it soon becomes clearly defined again.

Looking back towards the Menteith Hills

Lochan Allt a' Chip Dhuibh

- After 10 minutes, the path swings left (north) and meets a wall, passable by a stile. Here you have your first glimpse of the hills far to the north. After the stile you enter more forest with a clear path which twists as it descends.

- Soon you see a lovely lochan below, rich in vegetation and attractive to swans and other waterfowl. The path runs down along its left side, past a 'No Fishing' notice.

- Half way along the lochan, the path rises to meet a forestry road at which you will bear right. (If walking the Way in the reverse direction, don't miss the path down to the lochan: its signpost has long gone.)

- Before bearing right at the forestry road, cross over and climb a few yards up a small mound on the far side to reach a picnic table. This enjoys panoramic views of the hills to the north and Loch Venachar, with Ben Ledi and Kilmahog visible at its eastern end: see the title page photograph.

- Continue along the forestry road, which swings round the far end of the lochan and descends gradually through the forest. This consists mainly of conifers, relieved by some golden larch and several small waterfalls. On the way down, you pass a memorial bench to a local resident. After the car park, you leave Invertrossachs Estate through its East Lodge gateway.

- Bear right and follow the Invertrossachs Road along the south shore of Loch Venachar. Half a mile after the end of the loch, note the hump-backed bridge on your left.

- For Callander, keep straight on past the bridge, and after 1½ miles turn left to reach the middle of the village.

To by-pass Callander:

- At the hump-backed bridge, turn left to cross the River East Gobhain. Look up ahead and right to see 'Samson's Stone', a huge boulder perched precariously on the ridge above the road.

- Immediately after the bridge, you meet the A821 at a T-junction, where you turn right for Kilmahog. Walk along the left side of the A821 for less than a mile.

- Look out for the road sign 'Kilmahog, please drive slowly' and immediately turn left to pick up Cycle Route 7 which takes you to Strathyre (second bullet on page 42). The Cycle Route sign faces north, and is easy to miss when approaching from the south.

i

Rob Roy & Trossachs Visitor Centre

Combined Tourist Information Centre and visitor centre housed in converted church. The 'Rob Roy Story' (small admission charge) has talking head, audiovisual film and exhibition, with multi-lingual headsets. Open daily March to December (weekends only January and February), tel 01877 330 342.

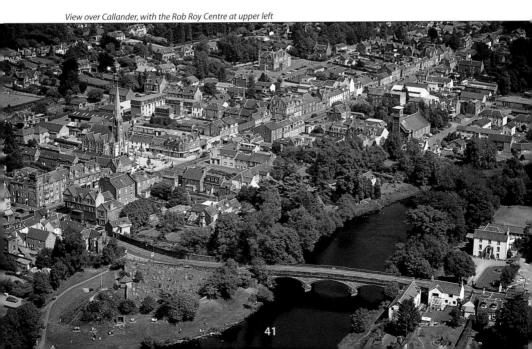

View over Callander, with the Rob Roy Centre at upper left

3·3 Callander to Strathyre

Map	**panel 2**
Distance	**9 miles (14½ km)**
Terrain	**good surface nearly all the way**
Grade	**easy, mainly flat Cycle Route, following the trackbed of a dismantled railway; mostly well drained, some tarmac but also some muddy bits**
Food and drink	**Callander, Kilmahog, Strathyre**
Side-trips	**Ben Ledi: see page 26**
Summary	**easy section shared with Cycle Route 7 along the west shore of Loch Lubnaig**

- Leave Callander by walking west along the main road (A84), looking out for the Cycle Route 7 sign. This follows the dismantled railway trackbed, with railway relics including signals, arches and old sleepers. The first mile is embanked over the river's flood plain, after which you meet the A821: cross it with care.

- From here, the Way follows the Cycle Route for 7½ miles all the way to Strathyre through splendid oak woodlands, with the still reflections of Loch Lubnaig on your right.

Loch Lubnaig – the 'loch with a bend'

Ben Ledi from Callander Meadows

- Walk upstream alongside the river Garbh Uisge. After heavy rainfall, it has fast-flowing rapids that culminate in the Falls of Leny. Rushing water drowns any traffic noise: be alert for cyclists.

- After the falls, you cross a minor road to the Stank car park. Keep straight on past the Strathyre Forest Holiday Cabins, unless you plan to climb Ben Ledi: see page 26. The river widens to become the southern end of Loch Lubnaig, 'the loch with a bend', often blessed with still, reflective waters.

- After about four miles, Loch Lubnaig ends in a spit of land deposited by the River Balvag, with a small lochan. This Site of Special Scientific Interest has outstanding riverine plant and animal life (e.g. azure damselfly and pearl mussel), and mixed woodland rich in bird life, including pied flycatcher.

- Descend gently to Strathyre along the minor road. Houses herald the approaching village. Look out for the marker post where you turn briefly right down a road between two houses. Immediately turn left and follow the path to the village centre. (To bypass Strathyre, see page 44.)

- Descend to and cross the suspension bridge, bearing left at its end. Cross a smaller bridge and pass along the back of a row of houses to emerge in the centre of Strathyre, where there is an information board, refreshments and accommodation.

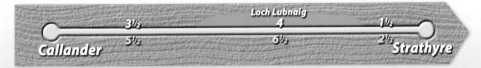

Loch Lubnaig

Callander — 3½ — 5½ — 4 — 6½ — 1½ — 2½ — Strathyre

3·4 Strathyre to Killin

Map	**panels 2 and 3**
Distance	**12 miles (19 km)**
Terrain	**good forest track or road as far as Kingshouse; minor road briefly, then good surface along Cycle Route 7 to Killin**
Grade	**fairly easy, maximum height 800 ft (250 m) with gradual climb and steeper descent into Kingshouse, followed by steady ascent up Glen Ogle and descent to Killin**
Food and drink	**Strathyre, Kingshouse, Killin**
Side-trips	**Balquhidder (Rob Roy's grave), Lochearnhead**
Summary	**a varied day, with pleasant forest views over the meandering River Balvag, then splendid views eastward to Loch Earn**

- From your accommodation in Strathyre, walk to the Munro Inn which is just north of the shops, on the east side of the busy A84.

- Turn into the car park alongside the Munro Inn to the small gate at the back leading into the Strathyre Recreation Ground. Immediately turn left on to a path that passes a former church (now a private house).

Alternative: by-pass Strathyre

About 75 m after the suspension bridge (last bullet page 43), bear right down a path. Walk through the car park (public toilets on the right) and cross the main road with care. Look for small steps at the right of a beech hedge that runs up the side of Forest Lodge. This leads to an informal path that climbs to a forest path where you turn left. Within a few minutes, the path joins the major forest road where you turn left and cross the large stream by a bridge. Within ten minutes, you rejoin the Way at the T-junction on page 45 (first bullet).

Kings House Hotel

- Within five minutes, the path meets a forest road at a T-junction. Turn left and continue uphill. (If walking the Way in reverse, don't miss this path: start looking just after the road makes a big hairpin bend.)

- Bear right and continue uphill, ignoring a road running downhill to the left. Enjoy the views across the valley to Ben Sheann (Beinn an t-Sidhein). After a while the forestry road levels out, and you see the River Balvag meandering through the valley of Strathyre below on your left.

- You start to descend, passing a quarry on your right. (Ignore a forest road that bears right uphill.) You may glimpse white buildings below and through the trees, but you have further still to go. The forest road veers north-east then hairpins south-west, losing altitude all the time, before swinging north towards Kingshouse.

- At the bottom of the forestry road, you meet the old A84 at right angles and turn right for the Kings House Hotel and Rob Roy Bar.

- From the hotel, walk underneath the new A84 on a minor road that, if you stick with it, reaches Balquhidder after two miles, where you can visit Rob Roy's grave: see page 16. To continue the Way, instead turn right just after the underpass at the Cycle Route 7 sign to Killin.

- The Cycle Route takes you parallel to the A84, rather close to it for the first two miles. Some streams help to drown the traffic noise in places, but it is a pleasant relief when the Route swings away from the road, soon crossing a large bridge across Glen Kendrum. A stone commemorates the young music teacher who died in 1997 while cycling on the A9.

- The Route starts to climb, gently at first, then steeply through a series of hairpin bends. The village of Lochearnhead lies well below you: for the diversion to visit it, see below. Otherwise keep climbing, enjoying the views of Loch Earn to your right. There's a picnic table part way up.

- Leaving Loch Earn behind, the Route veers left and enters Glen Ogle, towards its superb long viaduct. Soon afterwards, notice the ivy-clad bridge numbered 116, surrounded by mossy, dripping rocks. For more about this railway, see page 21.

Looking south down Glen Ogle towards Loch Earn

Diversion to Lochearnhead

Before the Cycle Route starts its steep climb, at a bridge under the old railway line, bear right through a gate and follow the path to reach a minor road. Bear right down the road which meets the main road at St Angus's Church. Turn left and walk north along the pavement for five minutes. At the main T-junction, turn right for the village.

After your visit, return to the main T-junction and continue north on the left side of the main road (now the A85). The pavement soon gives way to grass and you bear left up the entance to Lochearnhead Scout Station. Just past its big blue sign, look for the marker for Glen Ogle, where you bear right up a grass verge. Pass through the gate , across the fence and follow a waymarked uphill path, steep and muddy in places. When you reach Cycle Route 7, turn right to resume the Way.

The village of Lochearnhead lies near the Way

Lochan Lairig Cheile

- After another five minutes, notice the lochan on your left. This Site of Special Scientific Interest has rare plant life, including the Least Yellow Water-Lily, and rare sedges, mosses and bladderworts.

- Just after the lochan, follow the Cycle Route signs across the A85 trunk road (with care) to a car park with picnic tables and usually also a very welcome mobile snack bar. Continue uphill, soon passing a memorial to two RAF Tornado pilots killed while flying low here in 1994.

Memorial to the RAF pilots who died in 1994

- Walk through the side gate to continue the Cycle Route, ignoring the forest road that swings uphill to the right – unless you wish to by-pass Killin: see page 48.

- The Way now seems to descend towards the main road, but soon it veers away from the A85, and the walking becomes peaceful again.

- Before long, the tarmac surface ends at two bollards, and the Way curves to the right, becoming a pleasant forest road built up as a causeway in places. Notice the fine old stonework of the low bridges that carry you over the streams.

- After five minutes, at a T-junction the Way turns left downhill, and later turns right to pick up the trackbed of an old railway.

Falls of Dochart, Killin

- Enter Killin past the Falls of Dochart, a popular stopping place for coach parties. Note the restored watermill across the river (see below), and the South Loch Tay road to your right, where the Way leaves Killin. Cross the bridge to reach the centre of the village.

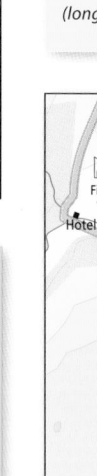

i Breadalbane Folklore Centre

Housed in a restored watermill, this Tourist Information Centre also has exhibits on Clans Gregor and MacNab (and holds keys to the nearby MacNab burial ground). The C8th Healing Stones of St Fillan are on display. Multi-lingual audiovisual; small admission charge; open March to October from 10 am to 5 pm (longer hours in season), tel 01567 820 254.

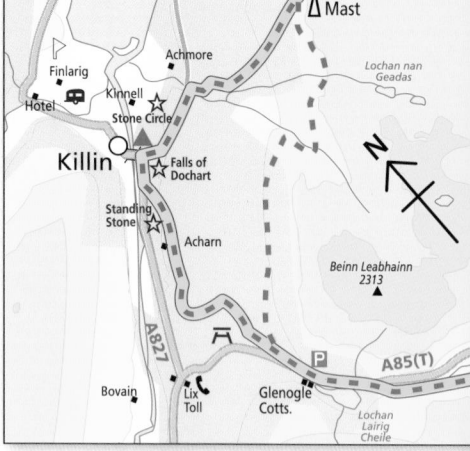

Alternative: by-pass Killin

Turn right up the forest road after the side gate (page 47), and follow it uphill for about four miles until you reach the tall mast west of Lochan Breaclaich (see page 50, third bullet). This saves several miles and a lot of ascent and descent, but means you miss the facilities and attractions of Killin.

3·5 Killin to Ardtalnaig

Map	**panels 3 and 4**
Distance	**12 miles (19 km)**
Terrain	**minor road giving way to rough track, followed by faint sheep paths, finally four miles of undulating minor road**
Grade	**long steady ascent to high mast (altitude 1900 ft/575 m) followed by long descent to Ardeonaig**
Food and drink	**Killin, Ardeonaig Hotel (lunch 12-2 pm)**
Side-trips	**Breadalbane Folklore Centre (see page 48)**
Summary	**a splendid cross-country section past Lochan Breaclaich with fine views over Loch Tay; compass useful; can be exposed in adverse conditions**

⚠ The cross-country route to Ardeonaig needs special care. Use the South Loch Tay road instead if not confident of passing though fields with livestock, if walking with a dog or if unsure of your compass skills. In season, check in advance for stalking: see page 61.

The Tarmachan ridge stands behind Killin

South Loch Tay Road

Killin — 9 / 14 — Ardeonaig — 3 / 5 — Ardtalnaig

- Pick up the South Loch Tay road (opposite the Falls of Dochart) and follow it for a mile to the Achmore Burn. Ignore the track just before the stream, but turn right immediately after the bridge. Its sign 'No unauthorised vehicles' is not obvious when the gate stands open.

- Follow this utility road as it climbs steadily. Soon you reach high gates: undo the S-hook and re-fasten it after you. If the gates are locked, use the ladder stile below and to your left.

- After the gate, look up to your right where a prominent mast stands next to another forest road. This is where the 'Killin by-pass' (see page 48) re-joins the Way. Divert briefly up towards the mast for a splendid view along Loch Tay to the north-east.

- The next mile or so is a pleasant, fairly level walk with forest on your left and fine views all around: look behind you for the twin mountains Ben More and Stob Binnein some ten miles away, often snow-capped until late summer. You may glimpse Loch Tay briefly, below and to your left.

- Soon you reach the impressive Breaclaich Dam. Made from stone from the quarry nearby on the left, this dam turned a small lochan into a major power source. It provides efficient hydro-electricity, driving three separate power stations on its way downhill.

- After the lochan, the track continues its eastward climb around the shoulder of Creag Gharbh towards a second, higher mast.

Lochan Breachlaich, a source of hydro-electricity

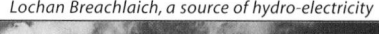

- From here, the track descends continuously, swinging north-east. Just after a tiny lochan to your right, you will glimpse Loch Tay in the distance. Start to look out for two clumps of evergreen woodland: your route takes you down to the lochside between them.

- Soon the track runs along a huge water pipe (part of the hydro-electric scheme). Within 200 yards, where the pipeline turns decisively south-east, turn left (north-east) to leave the track. Sheep have made various faint tracks all over the rough pasture: aim towards Loch Tay between the two clumps of conifers.

- At first, the Way is faint and discontinuous: just keep heading north-north-east downhill. Remains of shielings (farm buildings) soon confirm that you are on the right route. Look ahead for the buildings of Braentrian, surrounded by a few conifers, which mark where the road leads down to Ardeonaig.

The descent towards Loch Tay

- Descend towards the right-hand (eastern) end of the stone wall and go through the gate. From here on the path becomes clearer, and you cross a couple of fences (with care). The stream to your left has gathered force, and where the rough road fords the river there is a welcome wooden bridge. Keep well clear of all livestock, especially if they are with young.

- With the river now on your right, follow the farm track down until a small diversion takes you briefly uphill to cross the stone wall by a stile. This is to avoid the section of track that is in regular use for sheep mustering and is often gated off. After the stile, follow the line of the fence downhill and curving right to rejoin the farm track.

- Follow the road downhill past the Abernethy Trust Outdoor Centre. After a mile of very minor road you turn right at the Ardeonaig Hotel. This has a lovely situation facing the Ben Lawers group, and its bistro menu is available until 9 pm daily (tel 01567 820 400).

- Follow the South Loch Tay road for the final three miles to Ardtalnaig. At first you climb noticeably (to around 600 ft/180 m), passing the boundary sign for Perth & Kinross near The Old Manse. After some fine views of Loch Tay and the mountains behind, you descend towards Ardtalnaig.

- To take the Glen Quaich extension (see page 6), leave the Way at Ardtalnaig.

Ben Lawers dominates Loch Tay

3·6 Ardtalnaig to Aberfeldy

Map	panels 4 and 5
Distance	15 miles (24 km)
Terrain	tarmac at first, then rough paths and farm tracks, followed by gorge path with timber steps and boardwalk in steep parts
Grade	minor road at first, then steep ascent, followed by undulating ridge-walk (maximum height 1150 ft/350 m) and a long descent through the gorge; many tall stiles to climb
Food and drink	shop in Acharn, diversion to Kenmore, otherwise Aberfeldy
Side-trips	Scottish Crannog Centre; Dewar's World of Whisky, Aberfeldy
Summary	strenuous day with rewarding views from a ridge linking two fine gorges; could be split, e.g. by overnighting at Kenmore

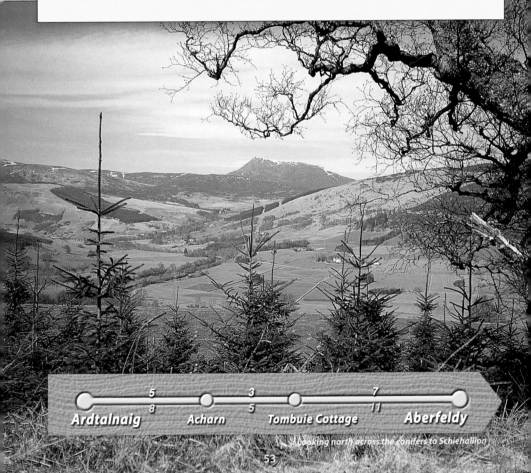

Ardtalnaig — 5/8 — Acharn — 3/5 — Tombuie Cottage — 7/11 — Aberfeldy

Looking north across the conifers to Schiehallion

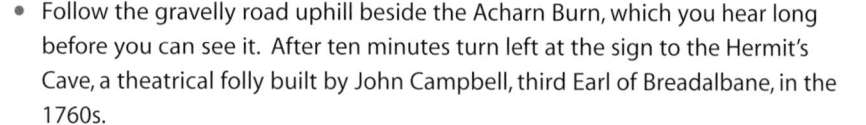

Looking south-west along Loch Tay

- From Ardtalnaig, the Way continues along the South Loch Tay road all the way to Acharn (about 5 miles/8 km). Unless your accommodation is in Kenmore, or you have a special interest in pre-history (see Diversion), turn right at the 'Falls of Acharn circular walk' sign.

Diversion into Kenmore

From Acharn to the Scottish Crannog Centre (see page 24) is 1.2 miles (2 km) along the South Loch Tay road, and from there Kenmore is just round the corner. To rejoin the Way, turn up the Glen Quaich road (with care) from its junction with the A827, then follow the steep zig-zags for a further 1.2 miles to Tombuie Cottage (see page 55).

- Follow the gravelly road uphill beside the Acharn Burn, which you hear long before you can see it. After ten minutes turn left at the sign to the Hermit's Cave, a theatrical folly built by John Campbell, third Earl of Breadalbane, in the 1760s.

Falls of Acharn

- Walk slowly inside the folly until your eyes adapt to the dark. Turn left to enjoy the glorious view from the platform. Originally this was enclosed, featuring a bow window overlooking the main falls, with stuffed wild animals in niches around the cave walls.

- After the platform, turn left to leave the cave by its upper exit. Continue up the road until a sign directs you left, down to the army-built observation platform. The timber walkways offer superb views over the cascades and the sculptured shapes in the smooth hard rocks below.

- Once across the falls, turn right uphill. Pass through the kissing-gate and left through the Remony Estate gate. Follow the farm road as it veers uphill, soon settling into an almost easterly direction.

- Within 1 km you cross the Remony Burn by a footbridge, passing through its gates and bearing left (northerly) afterwards. The path becomes indistinct for a while, but aim for the planks that bridge the small stream. After the gate, follow the broad track known as the Queen's Drive ever since Queen Victoria admired the fine open views of Loch Tay and Schiehallion from here.

- Soon you pass the farm buildings of Balmacnaughton on your left. Further on, a ladder stile marks entry to the Bolfracks Estate, where the path narrows through pleasant mixed planting.

- After a ladder stile, you reach the Glen Quaich road, where you turn right and walk uphill for about 700 m to Tombuie Cottage. Climb the metal gate at its left and follow the farm road for half a mile as it descends over a burn, past a shed, towards a patch of dense forest.

- You arrive at a tall forest gate, but do not enter. Instead turn right up a narrow farm track, passing through a gate into sheep grazing. Within two minutes the path descends to pick up a wide farm road. Follow it north-easterly, keeping the forest wall on your left.

- After the tall gates, the trees thin out and you glimpse Tower House below to your left. You emerge into a fine open section along a pleasant forest road with fine views over the Tay valley (strath).

Tower House

Looking south-east over Kenmore in winter

Taymouth Castle, until 1920 the seat of the Breadalbane family

- Below the Way, Taymouth Castle lies in the foreground. The castle dates from 1810 and was the work of several famous architects. Its interior is one of Scotland's finest neo-gothic examples, and it is surrounded by a golf course. The castle is being renovated to operate as a seven-star hotel.

- After this open section, you climb ladder stiles to pass through a deer-fenced section with clear felling to your right and patches of spruce on your left, with fine views over Strath Tay and the mountains to the north.

- Emerging from the plantation through a gate, you meet a minor road at a T-junction where you turn right. (If walking the Way in the opposite direction it could be easy to miss the left turn.)

- Follow the main forest road as it sweeps right and uphill around a tall pylon, where you pass through a gate and briefly head south. Soon you reach a Y-junction, where you bear left and continue easterly.

- After a mile you reach another Y-junction: the main track heads off right, but you bear left downhill under the power lines, soon leaving the forest over a ladder stile. The views open out and below you can pick out Aberfeldy and its Wade bridge: see page 58.

- Descend the grassy track past a large house (Upper Farrochil), passing under the electric fence if it's in place. Walk down the rough road almost as far as the renovated farm buildings at Dunskiag*.

* If you are seriously late or footsore, a shortcut is to descend all the way to Dunskiag and turn sharp right along its private road. This misses some fine Falls scenery and rough walking, and rejoins the Way just outside Aberfeldy.

- Just before Dunskiag, turn sharp right (south-east) up a track that soon passes through a gate. Follow it for 15 minutes until you meet Urlar Road, where you turn right.

- Within 50 metres turn left on a foot-path leading to the top of the Birks o' Aberfeldy (where the Glen Quaich extension rejoins the main Way).

- The Birks is a splendid wooded gorge formed over several millennia by the scouring action of ice and water. You walk it in the downhill direction only, making a dramatic, but not very strenuous, approach to Aberfeldy.

- There are paths down either side of the burn: turn right to cross a bridge, then descend its east side. The upper falls are dramatic when in spate. Lower down, just after a handrail section, notice Robert Burns' seat, where allegedly he wrote his famous song.

Falls of Moness, Birks of Aberfeldy

- Walk north along the A826 into Aber-feldy, Scotland's first Fair Trade Town. Visit its Tourist Information Centre and also the Watermill nearby: see page 58.

ⓘ Birks o' Aberfeldy

The birks (birch trees) are among many fine trees in this sheltered glen, with cataracts and falls set among craggy rocks. An information board at the lower end of the gorge explains its geology and wildlife. Robert Burns made it famous in 1787 when he wrote his song 'The Birks o' Aberfeldy'.

ⓘ Dewar's World of Whisky
www.dewarswow.com

Aberfeldy distillery, established in 1898, offers tours with tastings and audio guide (eight languages). An audiovisual presentation interprets the story of malt whisky. Café, e-postcard kiosk, nature trail and steam train. Open year-round (Sundays afternoons in summer only); tel 01887 822 010.

3·7 Aberfeldy to Pitlochry

Map	**panel 5**
Distance	**11 miles (18 km)**
Terrain	**long stretch of minor road, then uphill path with boggy bits across open moorland, finally forest tracks almost all the way**
Grade	**level road at first, then steady ascent (altitude 1150 ft/350 m) followed by moderate descent into Pitlochry**
Food and drink	**Aberfeldy, Strathtay (small village shop), Pitlochry**
Side-trips	**Visitor Centre and other attractions, Pitlochry**
Summary	**after the long road-walk, an ancient Right of Way through moorland and forest, past a stone circle, culminating in the centre of Pitlochry**

- Walk across the Wade bridge (see page 18) and immediately turn right down the riverside path next to the golf course. Near the road, cross the fairway with care, heading for the wooden gate.

- Turn right at the minor road and follow it for just over 5 miles (9 km). This two-hour stretch has no pavements: stay alert and face oncoming traffic.

- Notice the many fine mansions in prime south-facing situations, reminders of the heyday of large estates and gracious living. You pass Cluny House's Himalayan woodland garden and may wish to visit: open daily March-October, tel 01887 820 795.

- The long descent into and through Strathtay village heralds the end of the road walking. After the Golf Club and phone box, turn left up the 'Public footpath to Pitlochry' driveway. Once inside the golf course, immediately turn right uphill: the timber signpost is not obvious.

i

The Watermill
www.aberfeldywatermill.com

Atmospheric bookshop, art gallery, music and coffee shop housed in a sensitively restored Grade A listed watermill in Mill Street, Aberfeldy. This 4-star attraction was opened by Michael Palin in 2005. Open year-round (Sunday afternoons in summer only); tel 01887 822 896.

- At first, the walk feels pleasantly enclosed by dry-stone walls, with overhanging oak, beech and birch. You climb steadily, passing through various gates to emerge into open farmland with sheep grazing. Where the route appears blocked by gorse bushes, bypass them to the right, approaching the Tullypowrie Burn.

- About 20 minutes from Strathtay, just after a gate with stile, turn right over the footbridge across the burn, and continue uphill over a steep boggy bit. Turn right through the wooden kissing-gate, and maintain a north-easterly direction from here on across the open moorland.

- The path becomes indistinct in places, but continues to climb north-easterly, aiming for the corner of the forest (altitude 1150 ft/350 m). Pass through the remains of a gate in the fence, and notice two fine trees (Scots pines) standing on the right. Enter Fonab Forest by the tall ladder-stile at its corner. 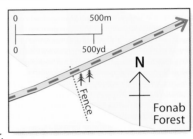 Pause to enjoy the glorious views behind you, all the way to Ben Lawers.

- Follow the forest road north-easterly, ignoring a left turn after five minutes. After a further 100 m, the four-poster stone circle stands mysteriously in a glade on the left. You can walk right up to these pre-historic stones but please do not touch them. The circle is about 5 metres in diameter, with fragments of its fourth stone lying on the ground: see photograph on page 60.

- Five minutes later you reach a cross-roads with a timber signpost. Go straight over on the narrow grassy path and follow brownish signs to Pitlochry via the Clunie Walk. At first the Walk passes alongside another forest road, then it crosses it, and descends alongside a burn.

- Emerge from Fonab Forest by a kissing-gate, and turn right to descend the minor road as it zig-zags downhill. Cross the A9, Scotland's main north-south highway, with great care (fast-moving traffic).

Clachan an Diridh stone circle is over 3600 years old

- Go straight through the gate down a minor road, soon crossing a larger road, angling left. Follow the sign to the hamlet of Port-na-Craig. Before turning right to cross the bridge, consider diverting straight ahead past the Festival Theatre to visit the dam. During May/June you can see large salmon in the viewing chamber: see below.

- Cross the River Tummel by its fine suspension bridge, which in 1913 replaced the ferry that had plied there since the 12th century. Its wobbles may be disconcerting, but it gives fine views and there's an information board.

- Cross straight over Ferry Road and follow a woodland path with timber waymarkers, leading to the car parks. Pass under the railway bridge, then turn right towards the Memorial Garden on Atholl Road, Pitlochry's main street. Turn right to visit the Tourist Information Centre.

Congratulations on completing the Way. Take a moment to reflect on all you've seen since leaving Drymen. Landscapes and lifestyles have changed profoundly since Rob Roy's lifetime.

i

Visitor Centre, Pitlochry

The dam and fish ladder centre has a salmon viewing chamber (admission free), an audiovisual 'The salmon story' and an exhibition about hydro-electric schemes (small charge). There are fine views from the dam walkway north over Loch Faskally. The centre opens daily (1000-1730) late March to late October and is operated by Scottish and Southern Energy plc, tel 01796 473 152.

Reference

Contact details

Phone numbers are shown as dialled within the UK. From elsewhere, dial the access code, then 44, then the number as below minus its leading zero.

Official website

Please refer to the official website before setting off. It contains a wealth of useful information on accommodation, transport and background, and is updated regularly:

www.robroyway.com

Stalking and the Way from Killin to Ardeonaig

During the main stalking season (September to November) there might be problems over walking the Killin/Ardeonaig cross-country route (pages 49-52). If the estate notifies any restrictions, they will be posted on the above website.

Tourist Information Centres

The Way is served by various Tourist Information Centres (TICs) run by VisitScotland (the Scottish Tourist Board). Some TICs also house visitor attractions, but we list them here by place-name. All have helpful staff who provide free information on accommodation and visitor attractions.

The TICs listed below are open at least six days per week, seven in summer, except for Drymen and Killin which are closed in winter, and Aberfoyle which is open at weekends only in winter.

Drymen	01360 660 068
Aberfoyle	01877 382 352
Callander	01877 330 342
Killin	01567 820 254
Aberfeldy	01887 820 276
Pitlochry	01796 472 215

Pitlochry walks

Perth & Kinross Council's leaflet *Pitlochry Walks* has maps of Pitlochry and walks including Ben Vrackie: price 50p from Pitlochry's TIC.

Notes for novices

Those who lack experience in long-distance walking may want to obtain our notes on preparation and choosing gear. Visit our website *www.rucsacs.com* and click *Notes for novices*. If you prefer, send a suitably stamped addressed envelope to the address at foot of back cover.

Service providers

C-N-Do Scotland
01786 445 703   *www.cndoscotland.com*

Transcotland
01887 820 848   *www.transcotland.com*

Walking Support
01896 822 079   *www.walkingsupport.co.uk*

The above offer support packages for walking the Way. In addition, Colin Welsh of **Bike & Hike** offers a baggage transfer service:

01877 339 788   *www.bikeandhike.co.uk*

Forestry Commission

The Forestry Commission is responsible for managing, protecting and expanding Britain's forests and woodlands, with the aim of increasing their value to society and the environment. From Drymen to Kingshouse, the Way lies within the Cowal & Trossachs Forest District, Aberfoyle, FK8 3UX (tel 01877 382 258). A specially highlighted version of the FC's *Guide to Queen Elizabeth Forest Park* showing the route of the Way, as well as Rob Roy's Cave on Loch Ard, is available from Rucksack Readers at £3.95 (inc p&p UK): buy online from **www.rucsacs.com**.

Transport

Traveline
08706 082 608   *www.traveline.org.uk*

Scottish Citylink (buses)
08705 50 50 50   *www.citylink.co.uk*

National rail enquiries
08457 48 49 50   *www.thetrainline.com*

British Airways
08708 509 850   *www.ba.com*

British Midland
08706 070 555   *www.flybmi.com*

easyJet
0870 6000 000   *www.easyjet.com*

VisitScotland has a website with a useful section of travel contacts, both for reaching Scotland and travelling within it: *www.visitscotland.com/transport*

There are about five direct buses a day between Glasgow and Drymen, journey time one hour. Services to Aberfoyle are less frequent and some involve a change at Balfron, journey time about 90 minutes: for details contact Traveline as above.

Pronunciation guide

Place stress on the syllable shown in **bold**. Visitors to Scotland often find the soft, aspirated ch sound (as in 'loch') difficult to pronounce correctly. Try asking a native to demonstrate, then practise the sound: this may provide innocent amusement all round.

Ardeonaig	Ar**dron**aig
Balquhidder	Bal**kwidd**uh
Breachlaich	**Braych**lich
Breadalbane	Bre**dawl**ben
Drymen	**Drimm**en
Loch Katrine	Loch **Kat**run
Quaich	Kwaich
Schiehallion	She**hal**ion
Stuc a Chroin	Stooch-a-**khroyn**
Trossachs	**Tross**uchs
Venachar	**Venn**achah

Development of the Rob Roy Way

Unlike Scotland's four Long Distance Routes, the Rob Roy Way has had no official support. It was developed in partnership between Rucksack Readers and Walking Support, a guiding and support company run by John Henderson. He also developed and maintains the official website *www.robroyway.com*.

Based on work originally done by Paul Milligan, Henderson was developing a route from Aberfoyle to Pitlochry with a major excursion through Glen Almond and Glen Quaich. Meanwhile Rucksack Readers had been working on a possible route from Milngavie to Pitlochry, using the West Highland Way as far as Drymen. Rucksack Readers and Walking Support joined forces in late 2001, and shared the development of a Rob Roy Way starting at Drymen.

The two routes were already similar except between Ardtalnaig and Aberfeldy, where one ran parallel to Loch Tay, whilst the other followed a long excursion via Glen Quaich. The latter has been retained as a possible extension and is covered on the *robroyway.com* website but not in this book. Over the next nine

months, we had productive discussions both with private land-owners and the Forestry Commission. We also met with both Stirling Council and Perth & Kinross Council, who are jointly involved in the maintenance of Cycle Route 7, the 215-mile cycle route linking Glasgow with Inverness.

Just after the Inaugural Walk in May 2002, the first edition of this book was published, and it sold out within four years. This edition has benefited greatly from valuable comments made by walkers, and many revisions resulted: see page 63. Please continue to send us comments on the book, ideally by email to *info@rucsacs.com*.

Martin Currie Investment Ltd has sponsored the first Rob Roy Challenge, a 55-mile bike-and-hike endurance event for teams fund-raising for charity. About 600 people took part in the first Challenge on 24 June 2006 and the event is set to become annual: see *www.robroychallenge.com.*

Further reading

Of the books recommended below, the first is Scott's classic novel, the rest are biographical.

Scott, Walter (2004) *Rob Roy* Penguin 501 pp 0-14043-554-9

Sinclair, Charles (2000) *A Wee Guide to Rob Roy MacGregor* Goblinshead 128 pp 1-899874-32-1

Stevenson, David (2006) *The Hunt for Rob Roy* Birlinn 339 pp 1-84158-483-5

Tranter, Nigel (2004) *Rob Roy MacGregor* Neil Wilson Publishing 192 pp 1-897784-31-7

Maps

For hill-walking, detailed maps are essential. The Ordnance Survey Landranger Series (1:50,000) covers the Way in three sheets (numbers 57, 51 and 52). The Explorer Series is at a larger scale (1:25,000) and takes four sheets: 347, 365, 379 and 386. As of 2006, OS is planning to show the line of the Way on future editions of both series, so check on this before buying maps for the purpose of following the Way.

Sustrans publishes the *Lochs & Glens Cycle Route North* showing the official Cycle Route 7 from Glasgow to Inverness (ISBN 1-901389-34-0).

Acknowledgements

The publisher is grateful to the following for co-operation over access, and for comments on the first edition: Captain and Michael Baillie-Hamilton, Niall Bowser, Andy Dunn/Scottish Water, John Henderson, Shirley Leek/Forestry Commission, Sir Robert Megarry, James Duncan Miller/Remony Estate, Paul Milligan, John Ogilvie/Paths for All, Perth & Kinross Council, Perthshire Tourist Board, Andrew Pointer, Athel Price/Bolfracks Estate, Scottish and Southern Energy plc, Mike Steward, Stirling Council, Sustrans, John and Helen Taylor and Andy Wightman; to all those who took part in the Inaugural Walk in 2002; to Rennie McOwan for rewriting section 2.1 on Rob Roy; and to all whose comments have made the second editon clearer than the first, notably Robin Budgett, Bert Hannah, John Henderson, Blair Hutton, Margaret Laidlaw, Maurice Lee, Peter Jackson, Jack Merriman, Rosie Merriman, Margaret Porter (C-N-Do) and Richard Sutton.

Photo credits

Barrie L Andrian/Scottish Crannog Centre p24; **VisitScotland Stirling** front cover (main), p10 (upper), p17, p37, p38, p41, p42, p44, p46 (both), p48 (upper), p52, back cover; **Forest Life Picture Library** (www.forestry.gov.uk) p27, p29 (both), p30 (both), p 31 (upper), p32 (lower), p33 (both); **John Dewar and Sons Ltd** p57 (lower); **Jacquetta Megarry** front cover (inset), title page, p4, p5, p8, p9, p10 (lower), p11, p14, p15, p16 (both), p19, p20, p21, p22, p23, p25, p26, p31 (lower two), p35, p36, p39 (both), p40, p43 (lower), p44, p45, p47 (both), p48 (lower), p50, p51, p53, p54 (upper), p55 (upper), p57 (upper), p58, p59, p60 (both); **Paul Milligan** p12, p43 (upper), p49; **Andrew Pointer/Transcotland** p18, p54 (lower), p55 (lower), p56; **RSPB Images** (www.rspb-images.com)/**Colin Carver** p28, **RSPB Images/Mark Hamblin** p32 (upper).

Rucksack Readers

Rucksack Readers has published books covering long-distance walks in Scotland, Ireland and worldwide (the Alps, China, Peru and Tanzania). Its 2005 series *Rucksack Pocket Summits* is for climbers of the world's 'seven summits'. For more information, or to order online, visit **www.rucsacs.com**. To order by telephone, dial 01786 824 696 (outside UK dial +44 1786 824 696).

ISBN 1-898481-19-9

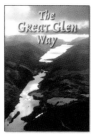

ISBN 1-898481-24-5

ISBN 1-898481-21-0

ISBN 1-898481-22-9

ISBN 1-898481-14-8

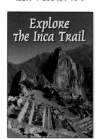

ISBN 1-898481-25-3

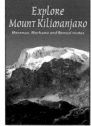

ISBN 1-898481-23-7

ISBN 1-898481-17-2

ISBN 1-898481-20-2

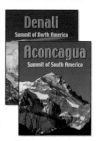

ISBN 1-898481-51-2

Index